LEADERS LIKE US
Pura Belpré

BY ANNETTE M. CLAYTON

ILLUSTRATED BY ELISA CHAVARRI

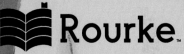

Rourke

Before Reading: *Building Background Knowledge and Vocabulary*

Building background knowledge can help children process new information and build upon what they already know. Before reading a book, it is important to tap into what children already know about the topic. This will help them develop their vocabulary and increase their reading comprehension.

Questions and Activities to Build Background Knowledge:

1. Look at the front cover of the book and read the title. What do you think this book will be about?
2. What do you already know about this topic?
3. Take a book walk and skim the pages. Look at the table of contents, photographs, captions, and bold words. Did these text features give you any information or predictions about what you will read in this book?

Vocabulary: *Vocabulary Is Key to Reading Comprehension*

Use the following directions to prompt a conversation about each word.

- Read the vocabulary words.
- What comes to mind when you see each word?
- What do you think each word means?

> **Vocabulary Words:**
> - *bilingual*
> - *citizenship*
> - *draft*
> - *folktales*
> - *gallant*
> - *inclusion*
> - *published*
> - *recite*

During Reading: *Reading for Meaning and Understanding*

To achieve deep comprehension of a book, children are encouraged to use close reading strategies. During reading, it is important to have children stop and make connections. These connections result in deeper analysis and understanding of a book.

 Close Reading a Text

During reading, have children stop and talk about the following:

- Any confusing parts
- Any unknown words
- Text to text, text to self, text to world connections
- The main idea in each chapter or heading

Encourage children to use context clues to determine the meaning of any unknown words. These strategies will help children learn to analyze the text more thoroughly as they read.

When you are finished reading this book, turn to the next-to-last page for **Text-Dependent Questions** and an **Extension Activity**.

TABLE OF CONTENTS

THE LIBRARY IS FOR EVERYONE

Pura Belpré was a librarian in New York City. Spanish-speaking children peered through the big glass windows. They stared in wonder at the children's section. Pura waved, but their parents tugged them along.

Their parents told them that because they did not speak English, the library was not for them.

Pura believed the library was for everyone. She would make them feel welcome. During story time, Pura decided to tell stories in both English and Spanish. Pura was a leader in **inclusion**.

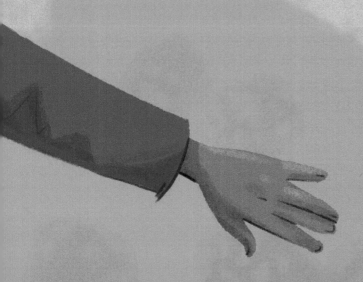

Pura lights a candle. The children are excited. The library's first **bilingual** story hour is about to begin. Pura's eyes sparkle. Her words are a paintbrush that bring characters to life.

The audience cheers. As story hour winds down, Pura blows out her candle. "Make a wish," she tells the children, "Pidan un deseo."

A FAMILY OF STORYTELLERS

Pura was born in Puerto Rico in 1899. She grew up in a family of storytellers. Her grandmother told her Puerto Rican **folktales**. Her favorite was about Martina, a very pretty cockroach, and Pérez, a **gallant** mouse.

In 1920, Pura traveled to New York City. The stories traveled with her. Like many Puerto Rican women, Pura found work sewing dresses. But it was not her dream job. She loved to read and tell stories.

A NEW LIFE IN NEW YORK

In 1917, President Woodrow Wilson signed the Jones-Shafroth Act, giving Puerto Ricans US **citizenship**. As a result, around 42,000 Puerto Ricans migrated to the US during the 1920s. Most of them went to New York City, creating the huge Puerto Rican population that Pura was part of.

When the New York Public Library needed Spanish-speaking workers, Pura was interested. She spoke English, French, and Spanish. The library hired her. Pura found herself in the wonderful world of books. She became New York City's first Puerto Rican librarian.

Soon, Pura noticed something.
There were no Hispanic children in
the library. Pura knew this needed to
change. But how?

As Pura shelved books, she looked for the folktales she heard growing up. The children would love those! But there were none. And there were no books in Spanish. Pura felt a deep sense of sadness.

Suddenly, she had an idea. She would **recite** the tales during story time. But the library told her no. There was a rule—you could only read from a book.

STORY TIME

Pura did not give up. She took a class on storytelling. There, she wrote her first **draft** of *Pérez and Martina*. She asked again for permission tell it. Finally, the library agreed.

Pura did not have a book to read from, but she had,

a talent for sewing...
...a paintbrush...
...and a dream.

In the quiet of her room, Pura painted puppets and stitched costumes.

Pura was ready. But she still needed an audience. Like paint in water, Pura spread her message throughout the Spanish-speaking community—everyone is welcome at the library. Bring your children!

The day of story time arrived. Pura hid behind the curtain. There was a big crowd. Colorful puppets danced across the stage. The children giggled with delight.

But Pura didn't stop there. She performed at schools. She ordered books in Spanish for the library. And she organized events for Latin American celebrations such as Three Kings Day.

As she told stories, Pura was also writing them down. She dreamed of becoming a **published** author. That way, Spanish-speaking children everywhere could enjoy her tales. Finally, in 1932, her book *Pérez and Martina* was published.

In 1940, Pura met Clarence Cameron White, a musician. Soon, they were married. Pura took a break from work to go on tour with her husband. Clarence played his music. Pura wrote her stories.

KEEPING HISTORY ALIVE

Pura published *The Tiger and the Rabbit and Other Tales* in 1946. It was the first English collection of Puerto Rican folktales published in the United States.

When Clarence passed away, Pura decided it was time to return to the library. While she was gone, others had continued her work. The library had bilingual story time. People of different backgrounds felt welcome. Pura helped make big changes to the library and her community.

In 1996, the Pura Belpré award was established in her honor. The award is given out annually to a Latinx writer and illustrator whose work celebrates Latinx culture in children's literature.

> **Storytelling is a living art, and each teller embellishes, polishes, and recreates as she goes along.**
>
> –Pura Belpré

TIME LINE

1899   Pura Belpré is born in Cidra, Puerto Rico.

1920   Pura travels to New York City for her sister's wedding and decided to stay.

1920   Pura begins working as a seamstress.

1921   Pura begins working for the New York Public Library at the 135th Street Branch in Harlem.

1926   Pura takes a storytelling course. She begins writing *Pérez and Martina.*

1929   Pura is transferred to the New York Public Library 115th Street Branch.

1932   Pura's first book, *Pérez and Martina: A Portorican Folk Tale*, is published.

1939   Pura becomes a member of the Association for the Advancement of Puerto Rican People. She helps establish the Archivo de Documentación Puertorriqueña, an early effort to collect original Puerto Rican documents

1943   On December 26th, Pura marries Clarence Cameron White, a violinist and composer.

1960   Clarence dies of cancer.

1968   Pura retires from the library.

1996   The Pura Belpré award is established.

1982   Pura passes away on July 1st.

GLOSSARY

bilingual (bye-LING-gwuhl): dealing with two languages

citizenship (SIT-i-suhn-ship): the condition of being a person who has full rights in a particular country

draft (draft): a first version of a document; not final

folktales (FOHK-tales): stories that get passed on from generation to generation

gallant (GAL-uhnt): heroic, brave, and respectful, especially to women

inclusion (in-KLOO-zhuhn): the act of including or making someone part of something

published (PUHB-lished): to have produced and distributed a book or other material so that others can read it

recite (ri-SITE): to say aloud something memorized in front of an audience

INDEX

TEXT-DEPENDENT QUESTIONS

1. What was the title of Pura's first book?

2. Why was Pura's work important?

3. How did Pura get into storytelling?

4. How was Pura a leader in inclusion?

5. Why did Pura tell stories in both English and Spanish?

EXTENSION ACTIVITY

Think about ways to make others feel welcome. Maybe you could invite the new student at school to sit with you at lunch, or ask someone who is alone at recess to play. Write your ideas down and share them with others to spread kindness.

ABOUT THE AUTHOR

Annette M. Clayton is an author living in Maryland with her twin daughters, husband, and one fluffy cat. Like Pura, she has Puerto Rican roots and hopes to share stories that will inspire children's imaginations, spark creativity, and foster inclusivity. One her favorite activities is hiking on the Appalachian Trail. When it's too cold for that, you can find her inside, drinking lattes and reading a good book.

ABOUT THE ILLUSTRATOR

Elisa Chavarri is an award-winning illustrator who strives to create work that inspires happiness, promotes inclusiveness and curiosity, and helps people of all different backgrounds feel special. She has illustrated numerous books for children including the Pura Belpré Honor book *Sharuko: El Arqueólogo Peruano/Peruvian Archaeologist Julio C. Tello*. Elisa hails from Lima, Peru, and resides in Alpena, Michigan, with her husband and two young children.

www.rourkebooks.com

Quote source: Marilisa Jiménez-García. "Pura Belpré Lights the Storyteller's Candle: Reframing the Legacy of a Legend and What It Means for the Fields of Latino/a Studies and Children's Literature." Centro Journal, Volume XXVI, No. 1, 2014, p. 123., https://doi.org/https://www.leeandlow.com/uploads/loaded_document/39/Pura_Belpre_Lights_the_Storyteller_s_Candle_Centro_Journal_Marilisa_Jimenez-Garcia.pdf.

Edited by: Hailey Scragg
Illustrations by: Elisa Chavarri
Cover and interior layout by: J.J. Giddings

Library of Congress PCN Data

Pura Belpré / Annette M. Clayton
(Leaders Like Us)
ISBN 978-1-73165-729-9 (hardcover)
ISBN 978-1-73165-716-9 (softcover)
ISBN 978-1-73165-742-8 (e-book)
ISBN 978-1-73165-755-8 (e-pub)
Library of Congress Control Number: 2023933227

Rourke Educational Media
Printed in the United States of America
05-1042511937